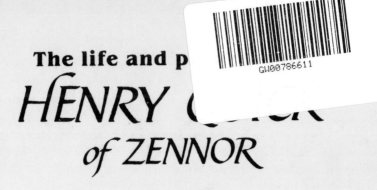

The life and p

HENRY Q̶̶̶̶̶K

of ZENNOR

Edited, with an Introduction and Bibliography,
by
P.A.S. POOL, M.A., F.S.A.
Past President of the Royal Institution
of Cornwall

TRURAN

Published by Dyllansow Truran - Cornish Publications
Trewolsta, Trewirgie, Redruth 216796

ISBN 0 907566 43 X

© P.A.S. Pool

Printed by Penryn Litho, Mabe, Penryn, Kernow

Revised and enlarged edition
1984

EDITOR'S PREFACE

The object of this booklet, like that of its predecessor of 1963, is to make available the verse autobiography of Henry Quick of Zennor, previously a work of such rarity that only one copy each of the author's first and third editions are known to exist, and none of his second. To this I have added a brief account of the poet, other examples of his work (including some not in my earlier edition), and a bibliography of his writings which includes several items found since 1963.

Apart from his autobiography, the main source of information about Quick is an account written in 1873 by Henry Nicholls, an eccentric Zennor man who had known him well; this was used by the late Walter H. Eva as the basis of a short account of the poet printed in 1933 *(Old Cornwall* Vol. II No. 5 p.36) and is now in my possession. Valuable information about the Quick family is contained in the papers of the poet's late kinsman, Henry Thomas of St. Just, to whom we owe the surprising fact that he was a cousin of Sir Henry Irving.

My best thanks are due to the following for kindly placing material at my disposal, for this and the previous edition: Mr. J.J. Banfield (Penzance), Mr. E.T. Berryman (Towednack), Mr. H.L. Douch (Truro Museum), the late Mrs. S.M. Eva (Nancledra), Mr. G.H. Harvey (Penzance), Mrs. M. Harvey (formerly of Penzance Library), Miss H.A. Ivall (St. Agnes), Mrs. E. Jewell (Penzance), Mrs. G. Kavanagh (formerly of Penzance Museum), Mr. C.J. Langman (formerly of Redruth Public Library), Mr. C. Noall (St. Ives Museum), the late Mr. C.R. Pengelly (Carbis Bay), the late Mr. W.R. Prowse (New Mill), Mr. Eric Quayle (Zennor), the late Mr. Ashley Rowe (Lostwithiel), Miss M. Rowley (Heamoor), Mrs. W. Thomas (St. Just), and Mrs. M.M. Uren (Heamoor).

P.A.S POOL
January 1981

INTRODUCTION

(The numbers in brackets refer to the verses of the autobiography, except those preceded 'Bib.' which refer to the bibliography)

Henry Quick, who was often called 'Henny,' lived for his whole life, from 1792 to 1857, in the Parish of Zennor on the north coast of the Penwith or Land's End peninsula of Cornwall, about six miles north of Penzance and five miles west of St. Ives. The parish, which is often said to be the most beautiful in Cornwall, comprises a narrow coastal strip of farmland bounded on the north by the cliffs and on the south by granite hills rising to 700 feet and more, behind which a plateau slopes gently down to the softer shores of Mount's Bay. This moorland plateau, dotted with granite rocks, ancient tin-workings, abandoned small-holdings, and the barrows of prehistoric man, is Henry Quick's country. Mill Downs, where he lived for most of his life and died, is a tiny holding on the most exposed part of the moor about a mile south of Zennor Churchtown.

Tradition states that the Quicks of Zennor and the next parish of Towednack are descended from a survivor from a shipwreck at Wicca Pool, Zennor, in about 1470. By the 18th century the family was firmly established in the district; the sundial on Zennor Church bears the date 1737 and the name of Paul Quick, and inside the church is a memorial to John Quick of Wicca, yeoman, who died in 1784 having in his life 'excelled his equals.' On present information, however, the poet cannot be claimed as a relation of these worthies, nor of Sir John Quick who was born at Trevega in Towednack in 1852, taken to Australia by his parents two years later, and who eventually became chief architect of the Australian constitution.

The poet's father, Henry Quick the elder, was born in 1754 (28) and on 28 January 1792 at Zennor he married Margery George, who was born in 1759 (74). He was a miner (4), but also 'leased a few acres of croft ground' (35) on Lady Downs, near the boundary between Zennor and Towednack parishes. His wife helped to 'keep the wolf from off the door' by spinning (4). Little is known of the elder Henry Quick's history before his marriage; Henry Thomas stated that Quick's father came from Little Tregenna in St. Ives, but according to Henry Nicholls both Quick and his wife were Madron people, and he came to Zennor shortly before 1789 to build a house and improve a farm at Concor (now Conquer) or Lady Downs. Quick had two sisters, one of whom, Jane Quick, married Hannibal Thomas of Zennor; they were the grandparents of the late Mr. Henry Thomas of St. Just, born in 1854, from whose papers most of this information on the Quick family was obtained. Hannibal Thomas's brother, William Thomas of Boswednack, Zennor, achieved fame by fathering (on two wives) a total of 23 children between 1801

1

Zennor

and 1841, and is remembered locally as 'Willie one-more.' Henry Quick the elder's other sister, whose name is not recorded, married a man named Behenna from Boskerris in Lelant; their daughter Mary married Samuel Broadribb, and their son was John Henry Broadribb, alias Sir Henry Irving (1838-1905), the great actor. Henry Quick the poet was the only child of Henry Quick the elder and his wife Margery, being born on 4 December 1792 (3) and baptised at Zennor on the 16th.

As a young child Henry Quick was weakly and suffered from fits (5) and at the age of six he narrowly escaped death from snakebite (9-19). Two years later he was sent to school (20), and showed some aptitude for reading, acquiring a number of books of which, after an early lapse, he took great care (25). He also learnt to compose rhymes (26). In 1805, when he was twelve, his father died (27), and at once the widow and son were faced with grievous poverty. The farm at Lady Downs proved too much for them, and had to be sold (37); they then moved, according to Henry Nicholls, to nearby Mill Downs. After five years they had to apply for parish relief (38), but Nicholls says that 'the parish on them no mercy shew,' and they were reduced to begging in the streets. Things were little better when Henry grew up; infirmity prevented him from obtaining regular employment, but he would do odd jobs for farmers and he and his mother would make brooms from heath and sell them around the district (45).

Eventually it occured to some kind benefactors that he could earn money from his talent for versification, and they had some copies printed for him to sell (48). His earliest printed work known is dated 1826 (Bib. 3), but the earliest recorded work is the poem written on the death in 1822 of his kinsman, William Thomas, the eldest son of 'Willie one-more,' and later included in the most celebrated of his broadsheets (Bib. 1, 13). Fortunately his verses proved popular, and for the rest of his life he would walk from parish to parish and town to town in West Cornwall, selling both his own broadsheets and also popular journals which he procured each month from Penzance. He soon became a familiar figure throughout the district, and when in 1833 J.P. Vibert of Penzance published a series of prints by R.T. Pentreath entitled 'Penzance Public Characters,' one was that of Henry Quick reproduced on the frontispiece. In 1842 an oil painting by Pentreath called 'The Zennor Poet' was awarded a bronze medal by the Royal Cornwall Polytechnic Society, but its whereabouts are not known. The only other known likeness of the poet is a rough woodcut, the block for which is now in Penlee Museum at Penzance, which was copied from Pentreath's print to illustrate the first edition of the *Life and Progress,* and was later reproduced in G.B. Millett's *Penzance Past and Present* (1880) and in the *Western Antiquary* (1883).

In 1834 Quick's mother died leaving her son, then aged 41, alone and virtually helpless in an unsympathetic world (71). Although he was receiving parish relief, rumours were spread that he had a hoard of money (80), and he narrowly escaped marriage to a 'loose and faithless she' who, however, scorned him when she found how poor he really was (84 - 87). But someone had to be found to care for him, and marriage - of a sort - was the solution. Henry Nicholls names the bride as 'Jane Harry, a maiden woman of 76,' a member of an ancient Morvah family, but it was in fact Jane Rowe, a widow aged 67 (24 years his senior) that Henry Quick married at Morvah on 25 October 1835 (91); probably her maiden name was Harry, and she was the Jane Harry who was baptised at Morvah on 2 August 1767.

In 1836 Henry Quick published his major work, the verse autobiography or *Life and Progress of Myself in Poetry.* The original manuscript is preserved at the Morrab Gardens Library in Penzance and is dated 15 September 1835 (also 'day 15, 624,' i.e. that day of the author's life.) A last-minute addition to the manuscript recorded his marriage:

> I've found a faithful guide through life,
> My dearest Jane, my loving wife;
> May we be joined in hand and mind
> To live eternal life to find.

This duly appeared in the first edition as printed. He originally intended to sell the booklet at 1d to the poor and 2d to the rich, but this interesting experiment in book marketing was apparently dropped and the *Life* was priced at 2d. It

3

must have been a reasonably successful venture, since a second edition was published at an unknown date, and in 1844 there appeared an enlarged third edition, still priced at 2d, the text of which is reproduced in this booklet.

It is to be feared that the marriage of Henry and Jane Quick was not happy, though it served its purpose of providing someone to care for him. Like her prospective predecessor, Jane apparently suspected that Henry had money hidden away, and became discontented when it was not forthcoming, so that the poet did not find domestic peace in his later years. He made no secret of this; the third edition of the autobiography omitted the verse quoted above, and instead included another (98) lamenting his 'eight tedious years of grief and strife' with Jane. Nevertheless they apparently remained together until she died at Mill Downs on 9 March 1855, aged 87, thus leaving him alone for the second time after nearly twenty years of marriage. The characteristic account of his end given by Henry Nicholls is very sad:

> For 4 years *(sic)* a widow's life his scanty meals so poorley able
> to fit and git. And so meanly feed that reduced his strength at
> last to keep his dying bead. Then a disgraceful neighbour did
> him tend to waste his 4 ton's of tatered collected book. And
> some do say was hurred out of time to rifle before his death of
> all he left behind. His pilgrimage was only 63 to 1855 *(sic)* and if
> was better feed I think much longer would be alive.

Morvah Church

4

One hopes that this was only slanderous gossip. He died at Mill Downs on 9 October 1857, aged 64, and was buried at Zennor on the 12th. The registration gives the cause of his death as 'Consumption (12 months)' and his occupation, rather sadly, as 'common labourer.'

One cannot claim that Quick's poetic work had any real literary merit or significance; indeed most of it is quite deplorable doggerel, though very occasionally poetic feeling breaks through. Its value lies in its vivid glimpses of life in West Cornwall in the last century. His greatest effort was the *Life and Progress,* a simple record of a sad and simple life; its very simplicity brings out with stark realism the plight to which poverty and infirmity reduced its author, so that we can better imagine that of others who lacked even his poetic talent to keep them above starvation level. Quick chronicles his varied woes with surprisingly little self-pity, and reflects on life's trials with patient resignation. Many verses are taken up with religious thoughts, and his constant theme is clear; the Lord knows best, and will provide. Simple faith and piety gave Quick strength to face poverty, illness, and the intrigues of 'secret foes' (80, 84). It would seem from his praise of the preacher 'Happy Dick' Hampton (55), and from references to the Methodists as 'the People of the Lord,' that Quick sought solace in chapel rather than church; unfortunately only the first line survives of his verses on *Church Division* (Bib. 39).

A glance at the bibliography shows that Henry Quick's main theme in his shorter works was Disaster, sudden death in its more sensational forms; he describes mine accidents, shipwrecks, suicides and miscellaneous catastrophes, concluding time and again with a cautionary reminder that sudden death is always at hand, and urging his readers to repent and be ready for their own ends. Most of these disaster verses concerned events within a few miles of Zennor; only rarely did more distant catastrophes engage his attention, such as a famine in Ireland, and a railway accident in Berkshire in which a Cornish clergyman was killed (Bib. 21, 22). Verses on less mournful topics are as rare, though he did celebrate the Coronation of Queen Victoria and the building of Pendeen church (Bib. 14, 24). One regrets that his character, and the tastes of the readers upon whose pennies he depended, obliged him to concentrate on doom and gloom to the exclusion of such themes as the matchless beauty of his native parish and the folk-lore of the Penwith peninsula (but see Bib. 40). It would have been worth much to be able to read the legend of the Mermaid of Zennor in the verses of Zennor's own poet, but we can only speculate on the morals which he would have drawn.

Another characteristic of Quick's verse is the acrostic; the autobiography ends with one on his own name (104), but others were written to record the names of his admirers (or sympathisers), such as those on John Verrant and Lucretia Harvey printed in this booklet.

It is tempting to compare Henry Quick with William McGonagall the 'Poet and Tragedian' of Dundee (1825-1902), hailed by *Punch* as 'the greatest

Bad Verse writer of his age,' whose verses show the same concentration on death and disaster and even bolder use of rhyme. The Scot's repeated rhyming of 'sorrow' with 'Edinburgh' is almost matched by the Cornishman's splendid effort in rhyming 'wedlock' with 'Boswednack' (a farm in Zennor, home of the prolific William Thomas.)

Henry Quick did not have the field of popular versification in West Cornwall to himself. Richard Williams of Sennen (1802-63), known as 'Blind Dick,' published his own *Life and Progress* in 1837, two years after Quick's first edition. Robert Maybee of Scilly (1810 - 84) wrote a prose autobiography as well as verses about shipwrecks. In 1863 C. Taylor Stevens, a St. Ives postman, published *The Chief of Barat-Anac,* a long poem about dreams and visions of the past at Zennor Quoit. After Quick's death others continued to write 'disaster verses' in his style, which continued to be published at least until the Levant Mine disaster in 1919, and both James Stevens of Zennor and Sancreed, the farmer and diarist (1847 - 1918), and his son of the same name (1876 - 1970), wrote verses in a style consciously modelled on that of Quick.

Henry Quick's keenest rival was Billy Foss of Sancreed, rhymester and stone-carver, and it appears that their rivalry in verse was accentuated by personal differences, Quick being religious and Foss a freethinker (Bib. 37). In 1929 Mr. R. Morton Nance printed an account of Foss *(Old Cornwall* Vol. I No. 10 p.6), and the following is extracted from a letter (now in Truro Museum) written to Mr. Nance by Henry Thomas of St. Just earlier in that year:

> I should add that Billy considered Henny Quick, the Zennor poet, was his strongest rival (by the way, Henny Quick was a cousin of my father's and I am named for him, as was Henry Broadrib also, whose mother was my father's cousin) and, whilst Henny Quick wrought the guide posts at Tregerest ('North Road') Choane and Brea (St. Just), Billy Foss did his best at Crows-an-Wray.

This indicates that the rivalry between Quick and Foss extended also to stone carving, but it is curious that Quick in his autobiography made no mention of being engaged in this trade. The three milestones mentioned by Henry Thomas as being Quick's work are dated 1819, 1833 and 1836 respectively, but it seems that he erred in attributing the first of these to Quick, and that it was actually the work of Foss (see C. Noall in *Western Morning News,* 8 December 1975).

Apart from R.T. Pentreath's print, and his own admission that he was 'not the handsomest of men' (44), there are only two first-hand descriptions of Quick. Henry Nicholls described him as having 'the most singular stature that I ever saw,' and said that he was very effeminate in manner and appearance, reserved and quite unfit for business, but modest and well-behaved; 'as a waterwheal that hast no stream that could not work, then took delight and self-taught both day and night to meditate and compose his pious books.' In *Cornish Notes and Queries* (1906, p. 279), a book compiled from contributions to the *Cornish Telegraph* newspaper, is a note signed 'H.R.' (probably Dr. Hambley Rowe):

> I remember him well 60 odd years ago, and he was known by the name of Henna Quick...... He was a very eccentric looking, tall, elderly man, and had a peculiar gait in walking, taking long strides, with a very ungraceful stooping forward at every step.

Henry Quick died as he had lived, in poverty and obscurity, and even in his native parish of Zennor was soon forgotten. One man who did remember him was Henry Nicholls, who in his younger days had been at times schoolmaster, grocer and proprietor of a horse-mill at Zennor, but who in later life became an eccentric and recluse, living at a tin stamping mill which he had built up the Foage valley. In 1850, as Overseer of the Poor of Zennor, he had managed to prove to the Guardians of Penzance Union that Quick's legal settlement was in Madron parish (whence his parents had come) and not in Zennor, from which parish he had been receiving 1/6d weekly relief for upwards of sixteen years. The poet does not seem to have resented this, for in 1852 he wrote four verse riddles for Nicholls (Bib. 29). In 1873, sixteen years

Eglosmeor Mill, Zennor

after Quick's death, Nicholls was asked for information about him by Mr. Henry R. Cornish of Penzance, but on making enquiries he found 'all the aged people gone dead and the young nearly forgot of what manner of person he was.' He sent to Cornish his own recollections of Quick in a document which is confused, incoherent and factually very inaccurate, but which is still of interest as giving a personal reminiscence of the poet, as shown by the extracts quoted above.

Henry Nicholls died in 1885, and thereafter Henry Quick might truly be called forgotten, although, quite astonishingly, he received the honour of an entry in the *Dictionary of National Biography* (Vol. XLVII p.99, 1896), being the only native of Zennor so far to attain that distinction. Certainly the parish has more reason to be proud of him than of its fleeting and unhappy association with D.H. Lawrence. Perhaps Henry Quick's best epitaph would be, not one of his own verses, but lines from Gray's *Elegy,* two of which he put on the title-page of his autobiography:

> Let not ambition mock their useful toil,
> Their homely joys, and destiny obscure;
> Nor grandeur hear with a disdainful smile
> The short and simple annals of the poor.

THE LIFE AND PROGRESS OF HENRY QUICK OF ZENNOR

(Bibliography 9, 11, 18)

PART ONE

1. My Christian friends, both far and near,
   Both high and low, pray lend an ear,
   While I my birth and life reveal,
   I trust your hearts will for me feel.

2. Henry it is my Christian name,
   And Quick of course by nature came;
   Old England is my native plain,
   God did create and me sustain.

3. 'Twas on fair Cornwall's north-west shore,
   On Zennor coast, December four,
   Seventeen hundred ninety-two,
   Born was I in this world of woe.

4. My parents they were honest poor,
   Just kept the wolf from off the door;
   My father laboured underground,
   Mother the spinning-wheel put round.

5. When I was but a little child,
   Convulsion-fits soon drove me wild,
   As teeth were cutting in my head
   I many minutes lay as dead;

6. Which surely gave me violent pain,
   Affected much my head and brain;
   My eyeballs did distressed roll,
   Whilst many laugh'd and thought me fool.

7. Nor did I seem to note or know,
   As other children mostly do;
   For I was in a sad strange way,
   My tender parents oft did say.

8. My mother of me took great care,
    Me hardly out of sight could bear,
    Whilst other little boys were free
    To play, I wanted liberty.

9. When I was in my six years old,
    A sad adventure I'll unfold,
    Happened to me one Summer's day,
    As I with mother took my way.

10. 'Twas through a croft, by the wayside,
    An adder in the ditch I spied;
    The thing did look so fine and gay,
    I felt inclin'd with it to play.

11. Quite ignorant and innocent,
    What by its speckl'd back was meant,
    I instantly my hand put down,
    To take it up from off the ground.

12. The moment I had done this thing,
    It sprang and stuck and pierc'd its sting,
    Which was so sharp and poisonous strong,
    Into the palm, and fast it hung.

13. My mother dear was sore affright,
    When she look'd back and saw the sight,
    It caus'd her to lament and cry,
    And said that I should surely die.

14. No, mother, if I die don't cry,
    I unto her did then reply;
    She straightway took me by the hand,
    And to a neighbour's house she ran,

15. Where she did show the dismal wound,
    If any cure could there be found;
    In tears she earnestly did cry,
    Their skill to try, lest I should die.

16. The poison had begun to fly,
    My hand, head, face swell'd dreadfully;
    An old man took a razor keen,
    The wounded place cut through the skin.

17. Blood, black as soot, did then appear,
    Then came the same both fresh and clear;
    Then milk and rinds of ash they found,
    And wash'd, and rubb'd, and dress'd my wound.

18. The swelling then did soon abate,
    And then my parents' joy was great;
    A surgeon next the same did view,
    Who said they'd done what's right and true.

19. Then physic next for me was brought,
    Which soon a perfect cure wrought;
    A purple mark doth always stand,
    Upon the back of my right hand.

20. When I was eight years old, indeed,
    Mother put me to school to read;
    Though slow at first I seem'd to take,
    Yet soon I did a progress make.

21. Of what I read, the greatest part,
    I very soon had got by heart;
    Borrow'd much books and read them through
    And bought a quantity also.

22. Many good people of each degree,
    Sev'ral fine books did give to me,
    And in the same I took delight,
    My constant study day and night.

23. Yet one sad thing I must reveal,
    When I had read them over well,
    The leaves I tore asunder, they
    Delighted me with them to play.

24. My father angry grew apace,
    He burned them before my face,
    Severely then corrected me,
    The folly of such tricks to see.

25. Soon after that I did reclaim,
    And much repented of the same;
    As careless then of books I'd been,
    So careful now of them I'm seen.

26. Chapters and stories could repeat,
    With every syllable complete;
    I likewise learn'd in little time
    To write, and then composed rhyme.

PART TWO

27. When I was in my thirteenth year,
    I lost my tender father dear,
    Consumption brought him down to death,
    And stopp'd at last his vital breath.

28. Just at the age of fifty-one,
    His glass was run, his life was gone;
    I trust the Saviour, all in all,
    Took pity on his precious soul.

29. 'Twas in eighteen hundred and five,
    April the eighth, he ceased to live;
    In T'wednack churchyard there doth lie,
    His dust to rest till the last day.

30. A favourite horse, call'd Punch by name,
    My father sold the very same,
    While he was laid on his death-bed,
    Ere his immortal spirit fled.

31. Poor mother then was left with me,
    In this wide world of misery,
    To toil and struggle up and down,
    Should fortune smile, or fate should frown.

32. But the all-wise, forever blest,
    Father and friend of the distrest,
    He by his providential care,
    Protected me and mother dear.

33. Glory be to his holy name,
    He was, now is, and ever the same;
    Mysterious are his works and ways,
    All things shall turn unto his praise.

34. When father died I had not learn'd
    One single penny then to earn;
    My mother by her toil and pain,
    Had me thus wholly to maintain.

35. My father, he, at Lady Downs,
    Leased a few acres of croft ground,
    And built a little cottage there,
    High rent thirty shillings per year.

36. Of which he small improvement made,
    Before he in the grave was laid;
    So poor and barren it became,
    Mother resolved to sell the same.

37. When two long years had rolled round,
    She sold the same for twenty pounds;
    A cottage, thirty shillings rent,
    Five years we liv'd in, till 'twas spent.

38. We then grew poorer every day,
    Were forced to beg some parish pay;
    From door to door went up and down,
    From street to street, from town to town.

39. Please to bestow your charity
    On a poor boy distress'd like me;
    Affected are my head and brain
    By fits, I oft-times did complain.

40. Some would take pity and relieve,
    Victuals and pence unto me give;
    But some again would nought but frown,
    Through envy strive to pull me down.

41. But bless the Lord, who kind has been,
    And led me by a hand unseen;
    O may I praise his holy name,
    And give him glory for the same.

42. I did to riper years arrive,
    And then some other means contrive,
    To earn my bread by industry,
    And not depend on charity.

43. When in my twenty-seventh year,
    Measles did then on me appear;
    When I was aged thirty-one,
    Small-pox my body over-run.

44. My stature it is five feet ten,
    Though not the handsomest of men:
    The great all-wise who formed me,
    As his good pleasure so I be.

45. We gather'd brooms and got them bound,
    And sold them to the country round;
    Who wants a broom? Be pleased to buy,
    I've got good ones, can you supply.

46. This calling though 'twas honesty,
    Yet evil ones would frown on me,
    Threaten and order me away,
    I should not steal the heath they'd say.

47. Sometimes a little job I found,
    To dig potatoes or break ground;
    Cutting of turf and peat also,
    A little I did sometimes do.

48. At last some good kind gentlemen,
    Took pity and did me befriend;
    Commended much my poetry,
    And got them printed off for me.

Making Brooms

49. My printed copies then did sell,
    And people seem'd to like them well;
    Parish to parish, town to town,
    I travell'd through and sold them round.

50. In selling books I took delight,
    Oft-times abroad to take my flight,
    And store my mind with subjects new,
    But let them be what's just and true.

51. Be pleas'd to buy my little book,
    And don't despise nor overlook;
    Please to take pity on poor Henny,
    I love to gain an honest penny.

52. And may the Lord my mind dispose,
    On worthy subjects to compose,
    That they may good examples be,
    And useful to posterity.

53. O Lord, on me, thy grace bestow,
    To learn and keep thy holy law;
    Sweet Saviour cleanse my soul from sin,
    Renew my heart and mind within.

54. Forgive my sins and follies past,
    And grant me grace while life shall last;
    The remnant of my mortal days
    Let me devote unto thy praise.

55. Let not thy blood be shed in vain,
    Dear Lord, let me be born again;
    Like Happy Dick* live humble I,
    And like poor Joseph† may I die.

56. O let me learn to be content,
    And not rapine at what is sent;
    In want or plenty, health or pain,
    Like Job may patience me sustain.

57. Like patient Joe‡ may I be blest,
    And count all things still for the best;
    Let me have lively faith in God,
    All things together work for good.

58. O let me have some good employ,
    My meat and drink thus to enjoy,
    However mean soe'er it be,
    O let me live by honesty

59. And unity and peace and love,
    That heaven may bless me from above;
    Lord, give me faith to call on thee,
    And from all evil set me free.

60. God's Sabbaths let me ne'er despise,
    But read good books, learn to be wise,
    Go to his house, and hear his word,
    Sing hymns, and pray, and seek the Lord.

*Richard Hampton, a travelling preacher.
† A London porter.
‡ A Newcastle collier.

16

61. A country life will suit me best,
    A city life's no peace nor rest;
    Such life will never do for me,
    A country peasant let me be.

62. On good potatoes oft I share,
    And barley bread my homely fare;
    Pottage and milk, most wholesome food;
    Bless God these things are very good.

63. Though some may slight and me disdain
    Should I of poverty complain;
    The Lord can succour my distress,
    He will not leave me comfortless.

64. Though some may laugh and at me game
    Nought else but fools would do the same;
    No laughing matter to despise,
    The mighty works of the all-wise.

65. Mocking is catching, it is said,
    Such thoughts should fill the mind with dread;
    They are not mocking at the creature,
    They're only mocking their Creator.

66. What sad examples have been shown,
    On many who were mockers known;
    Some wounded sore, or stricken dead,
    Or strengthless seized, or senses fled.

67. Lord, banish malice from my mind,
    To pride nor passion be inclin'd,
    Let me in love and meekness live,
    Learn to forget and to forgive.

68. My mortal age now fifty-one,
    Of fleeting years are past and gone;
    Let me my precious time redeem,
    In matters of the most esteem.

69. Now while as yet 'tis call'd today,
    How swift my time does pass away;
    I ne'er can call it back again,
    Lord let it not be spent in vain.

Churchway Stile near Zennor

PART THREE

70. Now, dearest friends, I next proceed,
Briefly for to relate with speed,
My mother's death, my marriage too,
And heavy trials I went through.

71. Twenty-nine years were past and gone,
Since my poor father's glass was run,
Eleven weeks likewise past by,
My poor old mother then did die.

72. The last seven years she did exist,
A cancer grew within her breast;
No surgeon's skill could her befriend,
This fatal wound her life did end.

73. Monday the twenty-third of June,
That morn her mortal glass was run,
In eighteen hundred thirty-four;
I trust she's safe on Canaan's shore.

18

74. Seventy-five years, and three months space,
    Were on this earth her mortal race,
    The latter years she did remain,
    Were spent in sorrow, grief and pain.

75. Her soul by death is called home,
    Her flesh consigned to the tomb,
    In Zennor churchyard underground,
    To rest till the last trump shall sound.

76. Then when the Lord comes in the air,
    O may we meet together there;
    O that will be a joyful day,
    All death, pain, parting done away.

77. Poor mother being dead and gone,
    I in distress was left alone;
    But the Almighty did me guide,
    And still he doth for me provide.

78. A good and tender mother she,
    No earthly friend so kind to me;
    My company by night and day,
    My head, and chief support, and stay.

79. A little country cot did rent,
    And struggled on with sweet content;
    Many-a-one prov'd friendly kind,
    And good to me, which cheer'd my mind.

80. But now came on sharp trials strong,
    Some secret foes did me great wrong,
    Their lying tongues soon spread around,
    That I'd got sav'd many a pound.

81. God witness be, I truth confess,
    One single pound I didn't possess,
    Should death this day my portion be,
    I've not enough to bury me.

82. I've found since mother's dead and gone,
    One trouble did not come alone;
    My near relations, verily,
    My greatest foes have proved to be.

83. They all forsook me in distress,
And left my mind quite comfortless;
Was any thing that they could gain
From me, they would have spar'd no pain.

84. Some secret foes commended me,
Unto a loose and faithless she;
.To whom I was by marriage vows,
To be the tender loving spouse.

85. Although our banns in church were call'd
The same for good was overrul'd;
I suffer'd full ten shillings loss,
Which was to me a bitter cross.

86. When she did view my humble home,
And found that riches I had none,
She quickly turn'd her back on me,
And never more my face would see.

87. But God, I trust, this trial blest,
And made all things work for the best;
Had she become my wedded wife,
It might have cost my precious life.

88. O may I never be dismayed,
Trust in the Lord, be not afraid,
To be my providential friend,
Whose love and mercy knows no end.

89. He did support me all my days,
To his great name be all the praise,
And sent many good friends to me,
When oft-times in extremity.

90. Bless God my health is very good,
I still enjoy my homely food;
O may I thank him for the same,
And bless and praise his holy name.

91. At forty-three I took a wife,
To be my guide through future life;
For I was very much distress'd,
Quite desolate and comfortless.

92. October the twenty-fifth day,
     Eight fleeting years have pass'd away,
     Since eighteen hundred thirty-five.
     I entered into marriage life.

93. My poor wife, she was born and bred,
     By constant toil to get her bread;
     Her mortal age, it now appears,
     Is just three score and fifteen years.

94. Although her strength is almost spent,
     Her mind is still on labour bent;
     But by the means of cruel foes,
     I have experienced many woes.

95. Uncivil treatment, most unkind,
     Has much destroyed my peace of mind,
     By means of strife and discontent,
     Through blame of what I'm innocent.

96. Cursed are those who maketh strife,
     And discord cause 'twixt man and wife;
     And such as easy do believe,
     A lying tongue will soon deceive.

97. Yet though by cruel foes belied,
     And my poor mind severely tried,
     The Lord above all things doth know,
     I trust his grace will bring me through.

98. Eight tedious years of grief and strife,
     I've suffer'd with a jealous wife,
     Her discontent torments me sore,
     Suspicious I have paltry store.

99. Display thy power, O God of might,
     My wrongs discover, and bring to light,
     By some wise means, through life or death,
     Before that I resign my breath.

100. Poverty is a grievous trouble,
      But harsh reflection makes it double,
      When poverty in doors doth hie,
      Out window love doth swiftly fly.

101. Content and peace is all I crave,
Nor noise or strife I wish to have;
My all-wise maker, ever blest,
Doth order all things for the best.

102. Though poor and mean should be my lot,
Let sweet content dwell in my cot;
Disdain no humble life to live,
With gratitude ask and receive.

103. Now to conclude what I have penn'd,
I trust the Lord will stand my friend,
And give me grace while here on earth,
And endless glory after death.

104. Has Envy Never Reigned? Yes:
Quite Unlike Is Christian Kindness.
Observe the same, remember me,
For here my name you plainly see.

THE DEATH OF PASCOE SEMMENS, 1826

(Bibliography 3)

Dear mortal friends and neighbours lend an ear,
A shocking accident I now declare;
How soon we're smitten by the darts of death,
How suddenly the Lord may stop our breath.

Poor Pascoe Semmens as for truth I tell,
Of Ludgvan Parish as 'tis known full well;
By lightning blasted, turn'd to silent clay,
And on the ground a breathless corpse did lay.

This awful shock on Friday afternoon,
Took place near four o'clock the ninth of June;
A heavy thunder storm from east did rise,
Dark foggy clouds did gather through the skies.

The morning fine and pleasant did appear,
The weather hot, the sun shone bright and clear;
For six weeks space there scarce fell any rain,
For want of showers many did complain.

Poor Pascoe Semmens that morning as we hear,
With cart and horses cheerful did repair;
From Trazza village he sets off with speed,
To Castle Dennis Downs he did proceed.

His father-in-law's own turves that very day,
To carry home intended was they say;
His brother-in-law John Hosking a grown lad,
Was mostly with him pitchman as 'tis said.

The morning passed on as we do hear,
At noon he home to dinner did repair;
And after dinner thus to be refresh'd,
For a short time compos'd himself to rest.

It was not long sweet slumber clos'd his eyes,
He suddenly was called to arise;
Some heavy showers threaten to descend,
'Tis best with speed our present work to end.

He started up just half awake 'tis said,
To downs then with all haste that could be made;
Dismal and gloomy did the sky appear,
And distant thunders were approaching near.

Having arriv'd and nearly made an end,
The threatening storm then downwards did descend;
Fierce lightning flashed, heavy showers did fall,
Loud claps of thunder roll'd from pole to pole.

He said to his young comrade, "Make haste drive on,
Dispatch with speed and let us home begone;
I'm wet to skin for every drop comes through,
More good those showers have done than we can do."

Just as he spoke those words and made an end,
A heavy shower of hail there did descend;
A dreadful thunder clap succeeds the same,
A blaze of lightning broke forth in a flame.

Poor Pascoe smote, fell lifeless to the ground,
By lightning struck received death's mortal wound;
One of the horses likewise kill'd stone dead,
The other also stun'd some time was laid.

His young comrade stood as we understand,
Four feet distance pitching some few brands;
Felt an uncommon stroke which knock'd him down,
Senseless some time he lay upon the ground.

He says as he was falling to the ground,
He saw both horses likewise smitten down;
Like one awake from sleep he lifts his eyes,
But finds himself unable to arise.

Poor Pascoe's naked body he espies,
Behind the cart-wain, as he cast his eyes;
At four feet distance from the cart he found,
Fallen on his back extended on the ground.

He tries but could not speak, when him he sees,
He then crawls forth upon his hands and knees;
Finds him a breathless corpse, was frightened sore,
His dear companion Pascoe was no more.

He left him there and straightway home did go,
And gave his friends the dreadful news to know;
They all mistrusted when they saw his face,
Some awful accident had taken place.

Poor Pascoe's corpse was home with speed convey'd,
On Sunday afternoon in dust was laid;
Coroner and Jury gave their verdict good,
"By visitation of Almighty God."

He aged was but twenty-nine last May,
He married was about three years they say;
A loving husband peaceable and mild,
A loving wife and only one sweet child.

He left his loving wife in tears to mourn,
Her dearest husband that will ne'er return;
"Little did I think," says she, "when out of door,
He took his leave to speak to me no more."

He useful learning from a child was taught,
To read and write most excellent was brought;
Cheerful and sober was as we do hear,
And duly did frequent the house of prayer.

Above two thousand persons there did come,
To see him laid within the silent tomb;
His loving friends did mourn for him full sore,
Alas! he's gone, poor Pascoe is no more.

His withered body in the dust must lay,
Until the last great resurrection day;
The trump shall sound, ten thousand thunders roar,
Shall cleave the ground and all the dead restore.

Loud calls around us from the Lord are sent,
And yet rebellious sinner won't repent;
God's awful judgment's through the earth abroad,
"Sinners awake! Prepare to meet your God!"

O sinner should the Lord in vengeance frown,
Where wilt thou run if justice cuts thee down?
Thy soul would drop into a burning hell,
Where none but damned souls and devils dwell.

Repent with speed and rightly be advis'd,
Before another thunder storm should rise;
If thus prepar'd no need hast thou to fear,
Though stricken dead shalt swift to heaven repair.

Now to conclude these lines and make an end,
Of these most awful verses I have penn'd;
Prepare, Awake, Seek Christ, Obey, Endure,
Strive Every Means Make Election Now Sure.

Rocks, Zennor Hill

JOHN UREN OF BESCROWAN, 1847

(Bibliography 20)

Our aged brother Uren is dead,
His soul has took its flight;
To dwell with Christ his living head,
We trust in realms of light.

A native he of Gulval was;
Born was on Christmas Day,
The day our blessed Saviour thus
Was born on earth they say.

In seventeen hundred seventieth year
After that blest event,
Our aged friend as doth appear
Into this world was sent.

In early days, from his youth up
He trod the worldly way;
Inclined to take a little drop,
Was merry, light, and gay.

Estranged was his heart from God,
And from his holy ways,
His holy name did rev'rence not,
Nor lived to his praise.

When he was nearly fifty years
Of age, he did begin
For to discern, as it appears,
The wretchedness of sin.

One night he had a horrid dream
As on his bed he lay,
Satan appeared unto him
His soul to take away.

With him he fought a desperate fight,
And could not from him flee,
Which waked him in great affright,
But Christ did set him free.

He joined the people of the Lord,
And learned to watch and pray;
His sacred church and holy word
Each blessed Sabbath day,

Duly attended and did read,
And strove with all his might,
By steadfast·faith in Christ, to seek
A city out of sight.

From all intoxicating drink,
For twenty-seven years
He did abstain, and serious think,
With true repentant tears.

Nearly nine years, as doth appear,
A widower was he,
Eleven children he did rear,
By care and industry.

Four now are dead, seven still survive,
Four of them married are,
In mortal life to toil and strive
By providential care.

The little farms he did possess,
His property and store,
Unto his children he has left;
On earth he'll be no more.

The last six months he did sojourn
Below, ere life expir'd;
He gave up family concern
And went to live retired.

Entrance grave Chykembro

About six weeks before his death,
He did converse with me,
'Twas the last time his face on earth,
I evermore did see.

He said above sixty years past,
He did remember well,
John Wesley preach at Geer, how Christ
The lunatic did heal.

Short illness closed his mortal days,
Death soon did lay him down,
Though constitution was always
Through life both firm and sound.

Upon the eighteenth day of March
In eighteen forty seven,
His soul did from this world depart,
We trust to enter heaven.

29

The day before he did depart
This life, he did reply,
"My work is done, Christ in my heart,
I'm not afraid to die."

Fifteen weeks fleeting space ran on,
Since our dear friend consigned
Was to the dust, when James his son
His vital breath resigned,

By short and fatal fierce disease,
Leaving in tears to mourn,
Six children and a pregnant wife,
Where he'll no more return.

We trust the Lord of life and death,
Who rules both earth and sky,
Hath took their spirits from this earth
To dwell with him on high.

THE DEATH OF JOHN MARTYNS, 1836

(Bibliography 12)

Mortals high and low, attention
Give to what I shall relate;
A most solemn scene I mention,
A poor young man's sudden fate.

Leaving his dear home one morning,
In the midst of life and prime,
Soon was locked in the bowels
Of the earth sent out of time.

Such untimely fate attended
Poor John Martyns called by name,
As he underground descended
And was crushed in the same.

This young man was bred a miner,
And did labour underground,
Where poor men ten thousand dangers
Constantly do them surround.

Born he was of honest parents,
And was always much inclined
To be of a meek behaviour,
Patient and contented mind.

His poor mother is a widow,
His poor father some time dead,
Ludgvan was his native parish,
Where he was both born and bred.

He was aged six and twenty,
Just about to take a wife,
In true love to be united,
And get settled through life.

Stout and tall in limbs and stature,
Strong and active, brisk and gay,
Full of life and health and vigour;
Soon a lump of lifeless clay.

'Twas December three and twentieth,
Friday morning just at ten,
Eighteen hundred six and thirty,
Did take place this solemn scene.

In the bowels of Wheal Tin Croft,
An old mine renew'd of late,
This poor young man he was labouring,
Where he met his sudden fate.

Down a shaft about ten fathoms,
Underground he did descend,
By the order of the captain;
Little thought his days to end.

A young lad descended with him,
William Curnow call'd by name,
Seven fathoms through a level,
Straight into a bolt they came.

Which was only eighteen inches
Square, about nine fathoms long,
On their hands and knees they creeped,
Only just could crawl along.

Then about a dozen fathoms
More, they through the adit came,
With a chain that they took with them,
Did take measure of the same.

They for sinking from the surface,
Through the level did intend,
A new shaft to the old bottom
Which stood at the level's end.

About forty years a standing
Choaked with water, mud and clay,
Which on their return from landing,
On poor Martyns broke away.

As 'twas known there was great danger,
He was charged to take great care,
Not a stone to move or meddle;
Yet he seemed void of fear.

As he struck some stones asunder,
Down the water, mud and clay
Soon did flow and filled the level,
With such force it broke away.

His comrade was got before him,
Through the bolt he just had passed,
When poor Martyns to him called,
"My both legs they are stuck fast.

Are you clear? I'm overtaken;
Let me on your legs lay hold;
Pull me out, I'm almost drowned,
Almost dead with wet and cold."

Curnow tried, but could not move him,
Though he strove with might and main;
Nine men tried their skill to clear him,
But alas, 'twas all in vain.

When they'd used their best endeavours,
And for him could do no more,
After all their toil and labour
They were forced to give him o'er.

Finding all means to deliver
Vain, poor Martyns he did say:
"Tis no use to strive, I never
More shall see another day.

Loose the ropes and take them off me,
Leave me where I am to die;"
Then upon the Lord for mercy,
He most earnestly did cry.

Farewell dear friends and relations,
Mother, brothers, sisters dear,
Farewell now to my dear Sally,
Farewell to all worldly care.

Brother could embrace a brother,
How affecting 'twas to see,
And conversed with each other;
Yet they could not set him free.

Fondly thus they strove to cheer him,
But 'twas vain for anyone,
Meat or drink then to bring near him,
For his appetite was gone.

When his life was just departing,
And was giving up the ghost,
His dear brother went in to him,
And he found his speech was lost.

"Brother, can't you now speak to me?"
He did cry and sadly grieve;
But, alas, he could no answer,
From his dying lips receive.

Near four hours space it seemed,
He his vital breath retained,
Death his spirit then released,
Though his body still remained.

Twelve days in deep mud and water,
Close confined underground,
Till they'd sunk a pit eight fathoms,
To the place where he was drown'd.

One o'clock on Wednesday morning,
And the fourth of the New Year,
Was poor Martyn's lifeless body
Loosed and taken out the mire.

Home to his dear habitation,
They his body did convey,
And his funeral procession
Was the following Sabbath Day.

To Ludgvan Churchyard was carried,
His poor lifeless lump of clay,
In his silent dust interred
Till the Resurrection Day.

'Twas reported near six thousand
Did attend him to his tomb,
Who in funeral rites most solemn
Guarded him to his long home.

His dear sole we trust is landed,
Safely on the Heavenly Shore,
Where all grief and sorrow's ended,
Pain and parting are no more.

Now to make a full conclusion
Of these verses I have penned,
Lord make this our resolution,
To think on our latter end.

Engine house at Ding Dong

ACROSTIC ON JOHN VERRANT OF ST. HILARY, 1835

(Bibliography 10)

Jesus thou bleeding lamb of God,
O wash me in thy cleansing blood,
Have mercy on my soul I pray,
Now lead me in the living way.
Virtue and inward holiness
Eternal God let me possess,
Ruin'd and lost by Adam's fall,
Restore me Saviour All in All,
A free and full redemption give.
Now guide me while on earth I live,
Then after death to Heaven receive.

ACROSTIC ON LUCRETIA HARVEY OF PENZANCE, 1852

(Bibliography 28)

Lord of all things who reigns enthron'd above,
Unto Thy Name be everlasting praise.
Celestial Being full of grace and love,
Righteous and Holy are Thy works and ways.
Everlasting Saviour Jesus All in All,
Take full possession of my heart and mind.
Infinite great physician of each soul,
An interest in Thy love I seek to find.
Hope, lively hope, and stedfast faith bestow,
A Crown of endless glory to obtain.
Reveal to me Thy just and holy law,
Vice to subdue and virtue to maintain.
Eternal life and endless peace possess,
Yonder with Thee to dwell in Realms of Bliss.

Rosemergy

WILLIAM THOMAS OF BOSWEDNACK

(Bibliography 13)

William Thomas, of Boswednack,
Father of twenty-three under wedlock.
All his family he did rear,
By industry, toil and care.
He has gained the highest prize
Of twenty-four parishes.
He is an example rare
Of diligence and godly fear.
May God bless him and his race,
Thus to spend their days in grace;
May their latter end be peace,
Heavenly joys that never cease.

Zennor Quoit, fallen

BIBLIOGRAPHY OF THE WRITINGS OF HENRY QUICK

This list, which is probably far from complete in view of the ephemeral nature of Quick's broadsheets, is based on those printed by Boase and Courtney in *Bibliotheca Cornubiensis,* Vol. II p. 541 and Vol. III p. 1320, with additional items located by me. Some of the titles are slightly shortened.

1. A copy of verses on the sudden death of William Thomas, Jun., a pious and happy young man of Boswednack in Zennor, who exchanged this state of mortality, to receive a glorious crown of immortality, 9 October 1822, in the 22nd year of his age. (See no. 13.)

2. Acrostic on the letters of the christian and surname of Anne Trembath, on the subject of the Lord's Prayer, 6 October 1823. (MS only, *Bib. Corn.)*

3. A new copy of verses on the melancholy accident and sudden death of Pascoe Semmens of Trazza in Ludgvan, who was killed by lightning in a thunderstorm at Castle-Dennis-Downs on 9 June 1826, aged 29 years. (Broadsheet in possession of Mr. J.J. Banfield; printed, slightly shortened, in this booklet.)

4. Churchyard spoil or human robbery exposed. A copy of verses concerning the late vile, base and unnatural deed committed April 1828 in a certain parish in Cornwall, by taking away a quantity of human earth out of the consecrated ground, together with a vast number of human bones and skulls, and putting out the same to dress and till the land. (MS only, *Bib. Corn.)*

5. A new copy of verses on the shocking accident and sudden death of two poor miners in Wheal Vor Mine, William Varker and John Arthur, aged 35 and 40 years, of St. Hilary and Lelant, on 23 May 1829. (Vigurs, Penzance; *Bib. Corn.)*

6. A new copy of verses, giving a full, true and particular account of the late melancholy accident and fatal catastrophe at Pendeen Cove, 2 October 1830. (Vigurs, Penzance; *Bib. Corn.)*

7. Death swallowed up in Victory. A new copy of verses in acrostic on the death of Thomas Henry Giles, a little boy, three years and four months, who was enoculated for the smallpox and afterwards fell into a vessell of scalding water, of which the dear child died much lamented, 13 April 1831. (MS at Penzance Library, which includes also "A Glimpse of

immortal glory: the child's dream, or infant girl's trance, composed by W.G.T.," in Quick's hand but evidently the work of another.)

8.   Two acrostics on Martha Glasson of Camborne, by way of Christian Advice, and by way of Prayer, 11 June 1831. (MS at Truro Museum.)

9.   Life and Progress of Myself in Poetry. (MS at Penzance Library, dated 15 September 1835, with some alterations and additions in another hand, which appear in the first edition as printed - see no. 11.)

10.   Acrostic on John Verrant of St. Hilary, 1 December 1835. (MS formerly in possession of Miss H.A. Ivall, now at Penlee Museum, Penzance; printed in this booklet.)

11.   The Life and Progress of Henry Quick, of Zennor, written by himself. (T. Vigurs, Penzance, 1836, price 2d, 8 pages, woodcut of author on front cover; copy in possession of Mr. Eric Quayle.)

12.   A new copy of verses on the fatal accident and death of John Martyns, a poor young man of Ludgvan, aged 26 years, giving a full account of his being suddenly stopped underground, and crushed in the bowels of the earth, by attempting to run an old shaft in Wheal Tin Croft Mine, 23 December 1836. (Huthnance, Penzance, booklet formerly in possession of Mr. Ashley Rowe; later reprinted by Riley, Darwen, broadsheet formerly in possession of Mr. W.R. Prowse, in which the victim's name is spelt 'Martins'.) Printed, slightly shortened, in this booklet.

13.   Broadsheet on William Thomas of Boswednack. This includes the verses on the death of William Thomas, Jun., presumably written in 1822 (no. 1, above); a list of 21 children of William Thomas, Sen., born between 1801 and 1837; an acrostic; a note on the Thomas family; and the verse on the family printed in this booklet. Later versions include the names of the last two children, born in 1839 and 1841. (Rowe, Penzance; later reprinted by Beare, Penzance, Saundry, Penzance, and others.)

14.   A new copy of verses on the glorious coronation of Queen Victoria, 1838. (R.D. Rodda, Penzance; *Bib. Corn.)*

15.   A new copy of verses on the fatal accident and death of Mary Carter, aged 38 years, wife of Francis Carter of Zennor, who was thrown from a horse against a sharp rock and broke her back, of which she survived but a few days and then expired on 31 March 1840, leaving a husband and four children to lament their loss. She joined the Methodist Society at Zennor in 1839, and found peace in Jesus. (Rodda, Penzance; *Bib.*

Corn.; copy by the late Mr. W.E. Stevens in possession of his daughter, Mrs. E. Jewell.)

16. A new copy of verses on a most melancholy act of suicide committed by a woman under temporal *(sic)* insanity, who hung herself at Boswednack in Zennor on 21 August 1840, with a brief sketch of the life of the deceased and the circumstances which led her to the perpetration of that horrid deed. (R. Kernick, St. Ives; *Bib. Corn.)*

17. Two new copies of verses. The successful fishery of the faithful enterprise, called The Gleaners; and the abundant season of 1840 contrasted with the scarce and gloomy season of 1839. (E. Paddy, Penzance; *Bib. Corn.)*

18. The Life and Progress of Henry Quick, of Zennor, written by himself, third edition, corrected and enlarged. (James Williams, Hayle, 1844, price 2d, 12 pages; copy at Redruth Public Library.) This includes additional material not found in the first edition (no. 11), and the text here printed is taken from it. The date of the second edition is unknown, and no copy of it has been traced.

19. Three Cornish Poems. Products of Cornwall; Penzance; Cornish Cantata. Additional lines composed by Henry Quick. (J. Williams, Hayle, 1845; *Bib. Corn.)* Among the papers of the late Dr. A.K. Hamilton Jenkin was a copy of a short poem by Quick on Mount's Bay, stated to be an addition to a poem by Rev. John Deane called *The Products of Cornwall.*

20. A new copy of verses composed on the memory of our late deceased neighbour John Uren, some years member of the Bible Christian Society, who departed this mortal life at Bescrowan in Gulval on 18 March 1847, in the 77th year of his age, together with some account of the death of his son James Uren, who survived him only 15 weeks and died 30 June, aged 41. (R.D. Rodda, St. Ives; broadsheet in possession of Mrs. M.M. Uren containing also two acrostics and some verses 'composed by a blind man on the scarcity and distress of the times;' another edition included in place of the last an acrostic on the harvest of 1847, *Bib. Corn.)* Printed, slightly shortened, in this booklet; verses 7 & 8 of the version here printed do not occur in Mrs. Uren's broadsheet and are taken from a copy made by Mr. W.E. Stevens - see no. 15 above.)

21. A new copy of verses on the scarcity of the present season and dreadful famine in Ireland, 1847, where many thousands are dying of hunger and pestilence. (J. Williams, Hayle; *Bib. Corn.)*

22. A new copy of verses giving a true and brief account of the late frightful and melancholy railway accident which took place at Shrivenham, 70 miles from London, 10 May 1848. (R.D. Rodda, St. Ives; *Bib. Corn.*) Rev. H.W. Phillips, Vicar of Chacewater, was killed in this accident.

23. An interesting dialogue between two schoolmates, Henry and John, 1849. (Harris, Hayle; *Bib. Corn.*)

24. A new copy of verses on the new church now erecting at Pendeen, 24 June 1850. *(Bib. Corn.)*

25. A solemn reproof and awful warning to scorners and mockers of the Almighty, which took place at Bumstead in Cambridgeshire last harvest, 1850. *(Bib. Corn.)*

26. The Brison shipwreck. A new copy of verses on the melancholy shipwreck and loss of life in the *New Commercial,* commanded by Captain Samuel Sanderson, seven men drowned near the Brisons on 11 January 1851. (T. Beare, Penzance; *Bib. Corn.)*

27. Acrostics on Sarah Fox Rowe and Emily Rowe of Penzance, 5 January 1852. (MSS at Penzance Library.)

28. Acrostic on Lucretia Harvey of Penzance, 5 January 1852. (MS formerly in possession of Mr. G.H. Harvey, now of the writer; printed in this booklet.)

29. Four riddles written for Mr. Henry Nicholls, 12 February 1852. (MS in St. Ives Museum; printed by Mr. Walter H. Eva in 1933, *Old Cornwall* Vol. II No. 5 p.37.)

30. A new copy of verses on the fatal accident and much lamented death of William Harry, a young man aged 28 years, who resided at Great Bossullow in Madron and met his untimely end whilst on a visit to his brother at Bunker's Hill in St. Buryan, where he was dreadfully wounded in the thigh by the ploughshare on 21 June 1854 and died about nine days after. (Copied by Mr. W.E. Stevens - see no. 15 above.)

31. This world is not our home! A new copy of verses, 1855. (F.T. Vibert, Penzance; broadsheet formerly in possession of Mr. E.T. Berryman, now of Miss M. Rowley; called 'The World is not our own' in *Bib. Corn.)*

32. Verses on the fatal accident and sudden end of two men drowned at Boscean Mine, St. Just, 11 February 1857. *(Bib. Corn.)*

UNDATED ITEMS

33. An awful warning to sabbath-breakers. A new copy of verses giving a full, true and particular account of the fatal and melancholy end of four men, Thomas Badge aged 34, John Harris Williams 24, John Beaglehole 21, and Henry Roberts 20. (S. Bennett, Marazion; *Bib. Corn.)*

34. A remarkable dream communicated by a friend, which he desired to have published as a warning to the world (in prose). (R.D. Rodda, St. Ives; *Bib. Corn.)*

35. A century days' calendar. (R.D. Rodda, St. Ives; *Bib. Corn.)*

36. A dialogue between a tippler and a tee-totaller. (Rodda, St. Ives; *Bib. Corn.)*

37. False accusations against Henry Quick by Mr. William Foss a freethinker. Falsehood detected and truth vindicated in answer to William Foss. (MS only; *Bib. Corn.)*

38. A brief memoir of Christopher Hosking. *(Bib. Corn.)*

39. Church division (commencing, 'When poor John Wesley did exist'). *(Bib. Corn.)*

40. The following verse, printed by William Bottrell, *Traditions and Hearthside Tales of West Cornwall,* Vol. I (1870) p.69:

> Our Cornish drolls are dead, each one;
> The fairies from their haunts have gone;
> There's scarce a witch in all the land,
> The world has grown so learn'd and grand.

Other titles available from

DYLLANSOW TRURAN

CORNISH BEDSIDE BOOK NO.1.
John Keast
Place-names, customs, dialects, remedies and recipes are nicely balanced by short essays and stories by early travellers, historical events and extracts from diaries. A throughly entertaining book.

Card Covers 9506431 8 1

VISITORS TO CORNWALL
Ida Procter
As J.C. Trewin says in his Introduction- 'Ida Procter can recreate her guests most surely... Everyone is here; Francis Kilvert for example, Ceila Fiennes is here - at St. Austell. Nearly two centuries later the young Beatrix Potter was arriving by train at Falmouth.

It is an enchanting book.'

Paperback 0 907566 27 8
Hardback 0 907566 26 X

HOW LONG IS FOREVER *Memories of a Cornish Maid*
Ethelwyn Watts
Born in the changing years of the decade that followed the First World War, the author describes her home parish as 'perhaps the most Cornish part of Cornwall' and she paints a word picture of a magical land.

Card Covers 0 907566 30 8
Hardback 0 907566 89 8

THE BOUNCING HILLS *Dialect Tales and Light Verse*
Jack Clemo
Jack Clemo says 'I contributed many dialect tales to Cornish Almanacks before the war capturing the lighter side of Clay country village life as it was 50 years ago. I have chosen eight of these stories, and have added a selection of my comic verse (not in dialect, but with a Cornish flavour). There are about 20 short poems, mostly written for or about children'

This is a book from a Cornish literary giant shedding a new light on Cornwall's own blind poet.

Card Covers 0 907566 38 3
Hard Covers 0 907566 39 1

THE HISTORY OF FALMOUTH
Dr. James Whetter
The author's considerable knowledge of life in the 17th Century Cornwall provides much new information about the origins of the old town - its growth over three and a half centuries and its social, cultural and religious history.

Hard Covers 0 907566 01 4
Card covers 0 907566 02 2